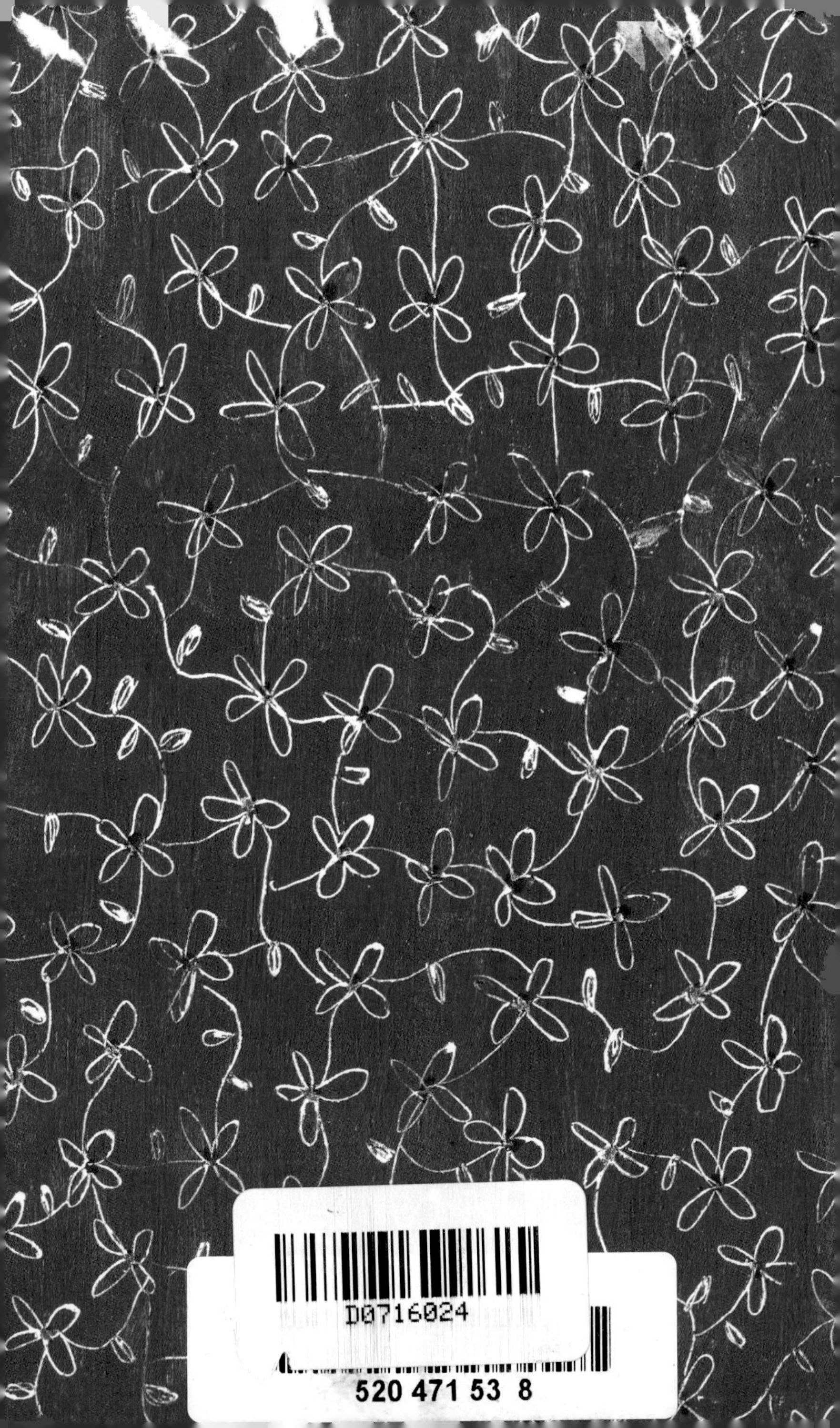
D0716024
520 471 53 8

I Am
A Woolly Hat

There are lots of Early Reader
stories you might enjoy.

Look at the back of the book or,
for a complete list, visit
www.orionbooks.co.uk

I Am A Woolly Hat

Salma Koraytem

Translation by Fatima Sharafeddine

Retold by Vivian French

Illustrated by Betania Zacarias

Orion Children's Books

Originally published in the Arabic language
in the United Arab Emirates in 2012
by Kalimat Publishing & Distribution
This translated edition first published in Great Britain in 2013
by Orion Children's Books
a division of the Orion Publishing Group Ltd
Orion House
5 Upper Saint Martin's Lane
London WC2H 9EA
An Hachette UK Company

1 3 5 7 9 10 8 6 4 2

ISBN 978 1 4440 0844 9

A catalogue record for this book is available from the British Library.

Printed and bound in China

www.orionbooks.co.uk

To you, the lingering fragrance of love, my mother, and Damascus, city of jasmine. Salma

There's something I don't understand . . .

What is love?

People are always talking about it.
They talk about it on the radio,
and they talk about it on
television – but I still don't know
what they mean.

Sometimes I wonder if love has
a shape . . .
Maybe it's long like
an elephant's
trunk.

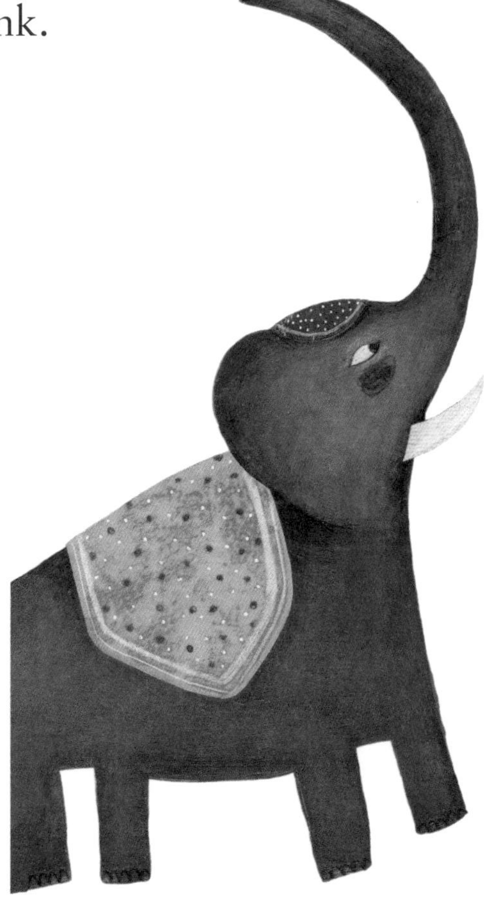

Or maybe it's short.
My lovely Grandpa has short white hair ...
perhaps love is short like that?

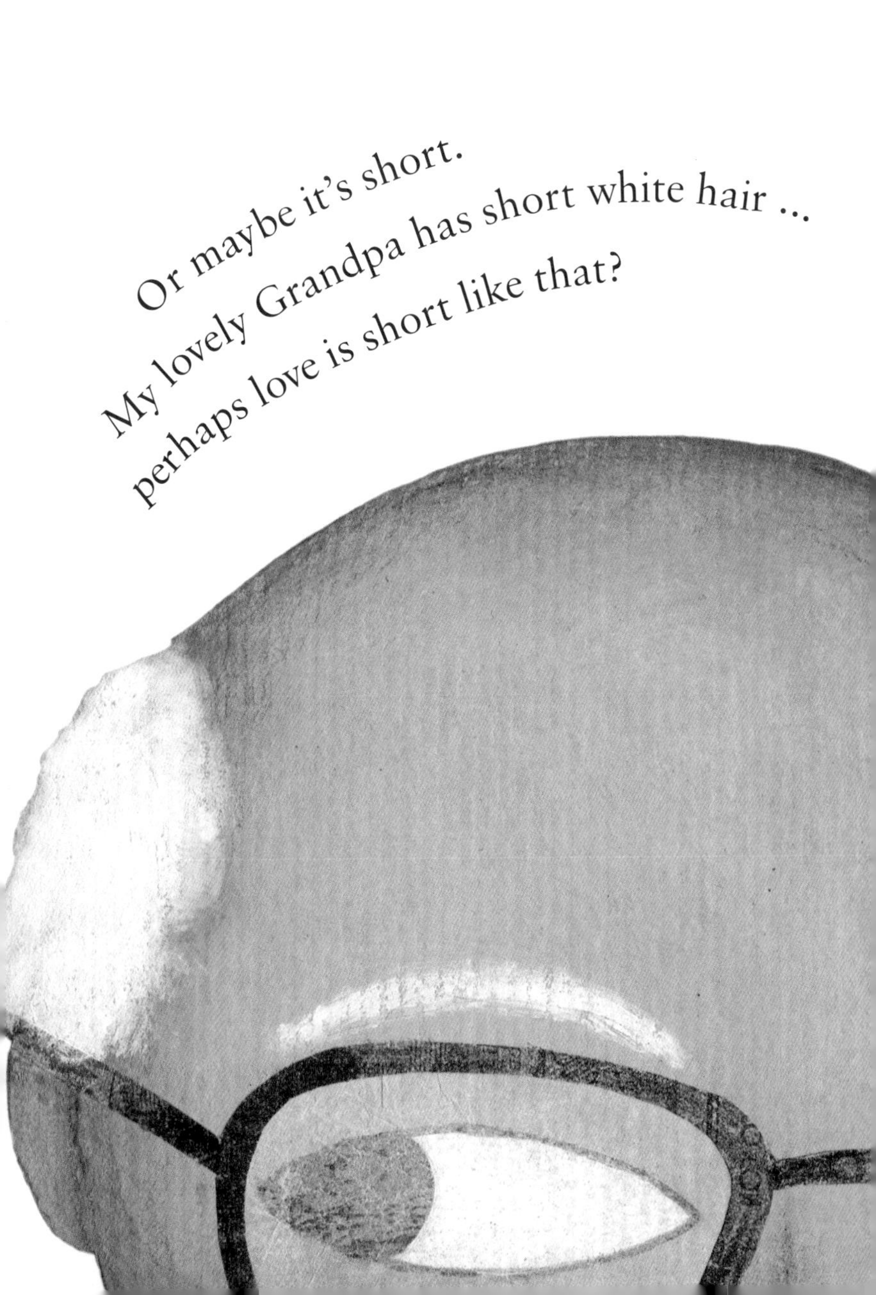

Could love be round and fat,
do you think?
Like my big round bouncy ball!

Or perhaps it's long and thin.

My mum cooks long thin
spaghetti.
It's one of my favourite meals.

But then again, maybe love
doesn’t have a shape at all.

Could love have a colour?
Love could be a beautiful red like
the roses in our garden . . .

. . . or it might be white, like the snow in winter. It's fun walking in the snow, even my little cat leaves footprints behind her.

Or maybe love is blue like the sky?
A summer sky, with birds flying
high in the clouds.

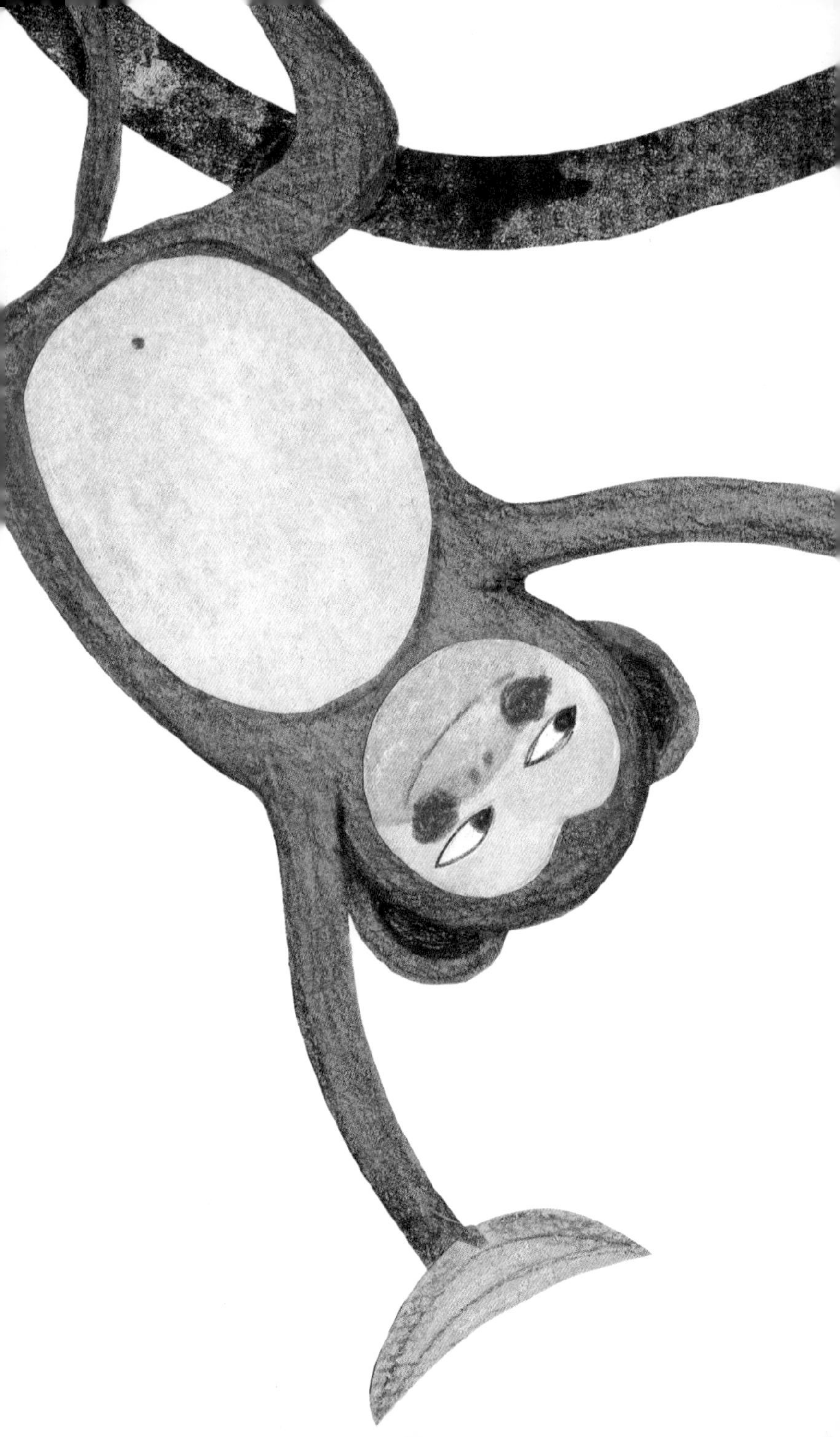

Or yellow, like bananas?

Love might be as clear as glass.
It might have no colour at all . . .

Maybe love has a taste.

I wonder if love tastes like the sweets in Grandma's jar?

Or it could be salty, or sour.
I don't think it would taste sour . . .
but it might taste like chips.
Crisp and golden.

Or love might taste like chicken,
or ice-cream . . .

but which flavour?

There are so many, I never know
which to choose. I usually have
strawberry, chocolate and mint.

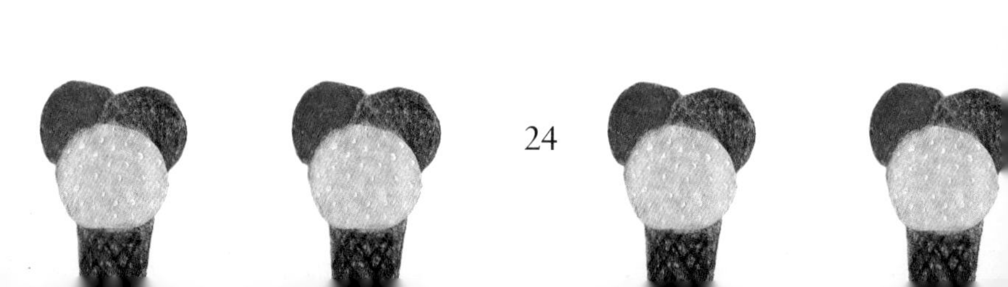

I get tired of thinking what
love might be like, so I
decide to ask Mum.
My mum knows everything.
Whatever I ask her,
she always knows
the answer.

Mum is busy tidying our clothes when I find her. "Winter's almost here," she says, "so I'm putting our summer clothes away and getting out our winter things."

"Mum! Mum!" I pull at her arm. "I really really want to know something. What is love?"

Mum laughs. "It's a little word,
Basma darling – just four letters!

LOVE

– but it means a lot.

I'd say that love is like the clothes
we wear in winter, the clothes
that keep us cosy and warm, and
protect us from the freezing cold."

I don't understand what Mum means, so I go to ask Grandpa. He is reading the paper, and Grandma is sitting next to him, knitting.

"Help me up, there's a dear," Grandma says, and I see Grandpa put down his paper. He holds Grandma's hand gently while he helps her up.

He smiles at me.
"What do you want, little Basma?"
I don't need to ask him my question.
I already know the answer.

"It's OK, Grandpa. I was going to ask you what love is, but I know! It's when you help Grandma and you look after her because you love her. You're like a woolly winter coat, Grandpa. You make Grandma feel happy and warm!"

Grandma nods. "That's right, Basma."

I leave Grandpa and Grandma, and run to find my big sister, May. "May! Can you tell me what love is?"

May is pouring milk into a bowl for our little cat, Sousou. Sousou is watching her, and purring loudly. She knows the milk is for her.

May looks at me in surprise.
"Don't tell me," I say. "I think I know. You feed Sousou and you stroke her because you love her. Do you know what you're like, May? You're like a cuddly cosy woolly scarf!"
Sousou rubs her head against May's hand, and purrs even louder. "Meeow," she agrees. "Meeow!"

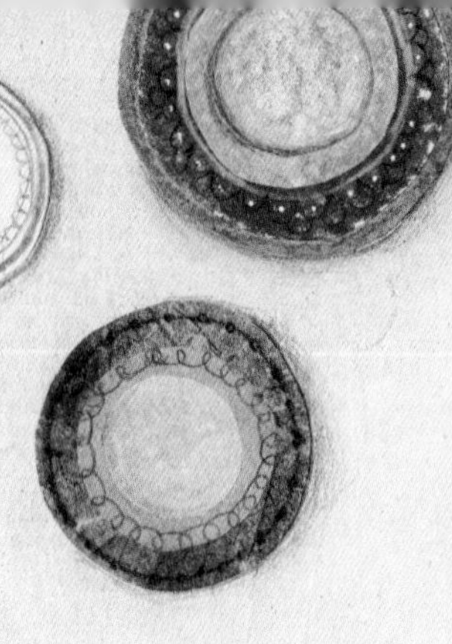

I leave May talking to Sousou,
and I run to find Dad.
Dad is giving my little sister
Maria a piggy-back. He is racing
round and round the room, and
Maria is waving her arms in
the air, screaming "Choo . . .
Choo . . . Choo!"

"Dad!" I have to shout, because Maria is making such a noise.

"Dad! Do you know what love is?"

Dad stands still, and opens his
mouth.
"Don't answer, Dad! I know,"
I say. "Love is when you play
trains with Maria, and race round
and round the sitting room.
You do it because you love her
so much. You're just like a warm
woolly jumper!"

I am feeling so happy that I go back to Mum. She is still sorting out our clothes, and I jump up and down when she sees me.

"Mum! You're right! Love is huge! It's enormous! It should be a much much much bigger word! L O V E isn't nearly big enough!"

VE

Mum hugs me, and says: “Darling Basma . . . All the letters in the alphabet aren’t enough for a word that means love.”
I hug her back, and give her the biggest kiss ever.

"I've just thought of something else," I say. "I love you, Mum. I love you very very much – that's why I hug you and kiss you. So – guess what? I must be a warm woolly hat!"

Mum laughs, and drops a kiss on the top of my head. "Quite right, my darling woolly hat."

And then I think of something else. I run into the living room, and turn off the radiator. We'll never need it again, because Grandpa is a woolly coat,

Dad's a woolly jumper,

May's a woolly scarf and . . .

I'm a warm woolly hat!

Basma is a warm woolly hat.
What would you be?

What would your family be?

What are you going to read next?

More adventures with

Horrid Henry,

or go exploring with

Shumba,

and brave the Jungle

and Arctic

with Algy.

Find a frog prince with Tulsa

or even a big, yellow, whiskery

Lion in the Meadow!

Tuck into some

Blood and Guts and Rats' Tail Pizza,

learn to dance with Sophie,

travel back in time with

Cudweed

and sail away in

Noah's Ark.

Enjoy all the Early Readers.

the orion star

Sign up for **the orion star** newsletter for all the latest children's book news, plus activity sheets, exclusive competitions, author interviews, pre-publication extracts and more.

www.orionbooks.co.uk/newsletters

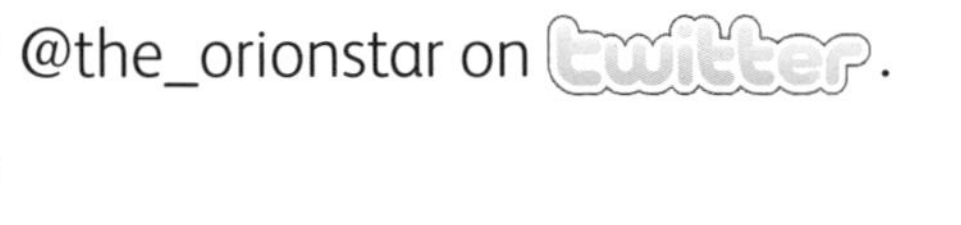